THINK RICH

ACT RICH

GET RICH

"Proven Principles to Acquire Financial Wealth"

THINK RICH

ACT RICH

GET RICH

"Proven Principles to Acquire Financial Wealth"

THINK RICH ACT RICH GET RICH

"Proven Principles to Acquire Financial Wealth"

First Edition / First Printing

Think Rich Act Rich Get Rich

Are you ready to begin an exciting journey to becoming
financially prosperous? Do you want to have confidence
in the financial markets? Do you need a practical guide
to help you navigate in becoming a very wealthy person?
If you answered yes to any of these questions, this book
is for you! Each chapter presents practical strategies to
help you achieve your financial goals. *"Think Rich Act
Rich Get Rich"* will take you on a practical journey to
help you realize your wealth creation ambition!

Dedication

To my daddy, Anthony T. Pleasant, who was a perfect example to me of what a man should be. I miss you so much and love you with all of my heart!

To my mother, Bertha Pleasant; you loved me so much and laid the foundation for my financial success! I can't wait to see you again!

To my pulchritudinous wife Kimberly, and my children Christian, Zion, and Nacara.

To my cousin/brother Robert Sumter. Thank you for being my lifelong best friend. I love you! To the New Zion Christian Church Family. You are a true blessing in my life!

Humbly Yours in Christ,

Apostle Jamie T. Pleasant

Getting the most out of

"THINK RICH ACT RICH GET RICH"

Congratulations on purchasing this book! Get ready to achieve a new level of wealth as you navigate and apply the practical principles presented in this text. This book is a culmination of my personal journey of increasing my wealth position in over 30 years!

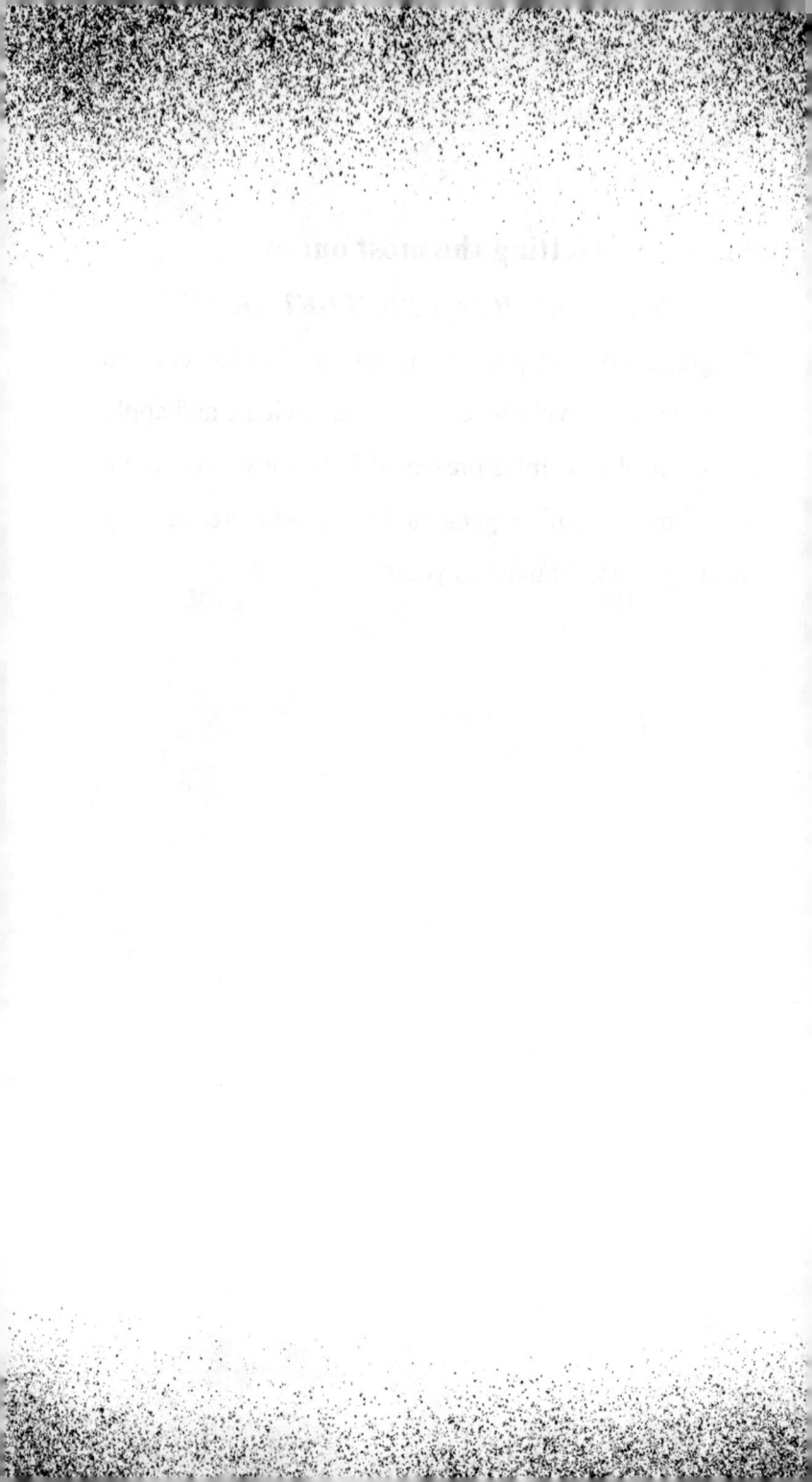

3 John 1:2 (KJV)
[2]Beloved, I wish above all things that thou mayest prosper and be in health, even as thy soul prospereth.

Table of Contents

Chapter 1

The Knowledge Principle

The words rich and wealth are bandied around all over the world numerous times each day. Some say that to become wealthy is not good and should not be the goal of anyone. Others argue that you will never be happy unless you become wealthy. The wealth debate has been continuous since the beginning of time. This book is written for those that have a desire to learn how to acquire and sustain wealth in their lives. What exactly is wealth? How does one become wealthy? More importantly, how does one sustain wealth that will become generational? These are questions that will be addressed in this book. First, it is important to know that the etymology of the word wealth is documented with origins in the mid-twelfth century and means a state or condition of happiness, well-being and joy. It is derived from the now obsolete word, weal. Weal means a state of being well, health wise as well as prosperous. Did you know that? Contrary to popular belief, happiness and joy are the foundation of wealth. It also means that one has obtained prosperity in abundance of possessions or riches. Looking further into the etymology of the word wealth, it connotes a state of well-being as it relates to health. Now, let me aggrandize the word wealth. First, wealth has a lot to do with happiness. Happiness is an emotion that we all display from time to time. However, one that is wealthy personifies happiness.

One that is wealthy personifies happiness.

In the 1520s happiness was defined to mean good fortune, as to reveal a pleasant and contented mental state of a person. Please note that happiness is a mental state that a person possesses internally, not what one experiences externally.

> *Happiness is a mental state that a person possesses internally, not what one experiences externally.*

In other words, happiness is a state of mind of an individual that is not dependent on anyone outside of oneself. Let's go deeper. This means that a happy person is an eudaemonic individual, capable of producing happiness from within.

> *A happy person is an eudaemonic individual, capable of producing happiness from within.*

Are you a happy person? Are you jovial? Are you pleasant to be around? Are you mad at the world? Are you always sad? Can you find wrong in anything? Can you find good in everything? These are some questions you need to ask yourself because wealth has a lot to do with how you project to others and how you view others. A wealthy person knows that things are never as bad as they seem! A wealthy person knows that there is happiness and joy in every situation! A wealthy person can change a negative situation into a celebratory event in the blink of an eye. In other words, wealth is a state of mind that is constantly in touch with happiness. That happiness produces wealth and wealth yields an abundance of prosperity that embodies the mind, soul and spirit.

> *Happiness produces wealth and wealth yields an abundance of prosperity that embodies the mind, soul and spirit.*

Now we must look at what prosperity means as it is the yield of happiness and wealth. The etymology of the word prosperity means to flourish and thrive in any condition with good fortune and success in anything good or desirable.

> *Prosperity means to flourish and thrive in any condition with good fortune and success in anything good or desirable.*

Wealthy people have a mindset and determination to thrive and flourish regardless of any challenge or obstacle they may encounter. Never forget that wealth is an inside job.

> *Wealth is an inside job.*

I will interchange the words rich and wealth throughout his book. Never forget that the words rich and wealth go hand in hand. It's also important to know that being rich or becoming rich is not something everyone wants to achieve in their lives. Some people are very satisfied with a status of living that doesn't consist of great financial and or material wealth. However, there are many people that aspire to become wealthy in all areas of their lives. The problem that many people face that aspire to become wealthy is that they have never been given the knowledge and training on just how easy it is to become wealthy. Have you ever noticed that there isn't a high school or college course on how to become rich? Why do you think that is the case? Well, it is because many want to keep the secrets to wealth to themselves and their immediate families. In the South, what we refer to as "old money" appears to circulate solely among its own kind. Never forget that. It's time to change this! Always remember that where there is no knowledge of wealth, there will always be a lack of it for those that desire to acquire it.

> *Where there is no knowledge of wealth, there will always be a lack of it for those that desire to acquire it.*

This book will teach you all about wealth in very practical terms. If you study and apply the teachings presented in this book in your life, you will acquire wealth. To be clear, wealth is not a difficult goal to reach if one has been trained correctly.

> *Wealth is not a difficult goal to reach if one has been trained correctly.*

You don't have to be a stockbroker, financial analyst, celebrity or professional athlete to acquire great wealth. However, you must possess good sense, wisdom, self-control, a happy state of mind and tons of patience! Therefore, study and master all the principles of this book and you will be well on your way to acquiring sustainable wealth that you can enjoy on this earth and pass on to the next generation of your family. Here is an interesting statistic. According to the Global Wealth Report (2024) and Fortunly (2025), there are only 1.5% of millionaires in the entire world. And 88% of them have a college degree. The United States only comprises 6.7% of millionaires in the entire population. Interestingly, 76% of American millionaires are White and only 8% are African American. The average net worth of millionaires in America is $2.2 Million (Forbes 2023). And even more interestingly, is the fact that on average, it took them 32 years to become a millionaire. Again, patience and discipline are the keys to becoming wealthy. The rich mindset knows that it takes discipline and patience to become a millionaire.

Reflection

1. What is wealth?

_____

_____

_____

_____

_____

2. What type of mental state must you be in to possess wealth? And, why should you have such a persona?

_____

_____

_____

_____

_____

_____

3. Write your goals for acquiring wealth.

_____

_____

_____

_____

_____

_____

Chapter 2

The Pleasant Principle

One of the easiest and surest ways to become wealthy is to be married and live off of one salary and invest the entire salary in the equity markets. This is simply called the *"Pleasant Principle."* I actually taught this principle in one of my classes where I serve as a professor and one of my prized students told me that he uses it in his personal life to this very day. My former student, who I will only give his initials N.W., told me that one day someone asked him where he learned about living off of one salary and he replied that I had shared with him this knowledge and that he called it the *"Pleasant Principle!"* So now you know where this principle came from and why it is named as such. The *"Pleasant Principle"* requires that you leverage one salary to contribute to your financial goal of accumulating great wealth. Let's say for example, a husband and wife both have stable incomes. The wife makes $50,000 and the husband makes $52,800. That's a total income of $102,800. Instead of getting in debt and buying expensive things, they can decide to live off of one salary. So then, in this example, if they decide to live off of the $52,800 salary that the husband makes, that would be a great step in creating wealth for their family. Think about this for a minute. Can anyone live off of $52,800 a year? You better believe they can. The median total household income for African Americans in 2023 according to the Pew

Research Center was $54,000 per capita. Please note that $54,000 is for the entire family. That is four people including children. Now, if four people can live off of $54,000, surely two people working with a total household salary of $102,800 can live off of $52,800. Therefore, if you really look at these numbers, you can see that you can develop a plan to live off one income and be very successful on your way to accumulating wealth. For example, let's look back at our income example above, If this couple decides to live off of $52,800 and invested $45,000 ($3750 monthly) after taxes etc. in securities with an average return of 10% in the S&P 500 ETF or mutual fund security, in 5 years they would have $295,433! Let's look at one more scenario. Let's say they did that for 10 years. Guess what, they would have $765,193. That's right! They could consider themselves on their way to becoming millionaires! Are you planning on being around for 10 years? Can you see yourself being disciplined enough to budget your income and expenses for 10 years? I think

you can. That's very doable and can be done in this short period of time. But, I have a secret to share with you. For those that I have personally known to have set this structure of their finances, they have reached their dollar goal amount in a much faster time. Honestly, it just happens that way. Once you make your mind up to invest and grow your money, great things begin to happen to you in order for you to reach your goal. You may ask, how can we live off of one income and be happy? Simple. Instead of paying on a new car or two new cars. Pay cash for an older car that is very inexpensive but reliable. Share one car. Or buy two reliable cars and pay cash for them. Next, rent a nice apartment that is inexpensive but livable. You don't have to rush and buy a house if you are newly married. Remember, in a few years under your new investment plan, you will be able to buy a very nice house. Oh, and don't have any children until you have reached your financial goal that you have set. Seriously, they will take all of your money!

Reflection Questions

1. What is the best way for married couples to become wealthy in a few years?

_____

_____

_____

_____

_____

_____

2. Set a goal for you and your mate about how much money you would like to have and how long it will take you to get it.

_____

_____

_____

_____

_____

_____

_____

_____

3. Below, write the adjustments you will make in order to be sure you reach your financial goals.

_____

_____

_____

_____

_____

_____

4. Write down things you must stop doing in order for you to reach your wealth goals.

_____

_____

_____

_____

_____

_____

_____

_____

Chapter 3

The Goodwill Principle

The goodwill principle is one that I have practiced ever since I was in college as an undergraduate student and had limited means of income. I would make sure that I would go to the very wealthy and affluent goodwill stores that were located close to where I was living. You would be surprised at the quality of merchandise that's available as far as clothing is concerned at goodwill stores in affluent neighborhoods. Most people that are wealthy will cycle through their clothes seasonally and replenish them with the latest fashions. Therefore, what I would do is I would always go to the goodwill stores at certain times of the year and I was able to get designer name suits between $10 and $15. That is correct. I would pay a fraction of the cost that the original purchaser paid for these expensive items and I would look rich. That is the key if your mindset is one that is of an affluent person. You should be able to dress the part even if you haven't achieved that particular status yet. A rich mindset is never limited to the amount of money that he or she does not have. A rich mindset is very resourceful and can take a little and make it look like a lot. A rich mindset can take a bargain and make it look like a jewel. A rich mindset can take simple things and make them look luxurious. Goodwill stores are an excellent place to be able to purchase recycled goods that the affluent have no need for anymore. You will be surprised of the name brands you will find in clothing at goodwill stores. You will even find custom made men and women's suits. That will make you look as if you have spent hundreds if not thousands of dollars for what you are wearing when others see you. Again, it is about the mindset and it is all about the image that you are portraying and how you want others to view you. The way you present yourself will have a direct impact on how people perceive you. There's nothing fake or phony about being smart and shrewd when it comes to purchasing quality recycled goods from a goodwill store that is located in an affluent community. I remember once when I shopped at a goodwill store, I purchased three Brooks Brothers suits in the 1990s for a total of $25. That is correct $25. I immediately took them to the local cleaners and had them sanitized, pressed, and began to wear them at all of my interviews that were scheduled during my last semester during my undergraduate college years. I remember one of my interviewers, a male, asking me where I got my fancy clothing and if they were custom made. I instantly answered, telling

him that the suit I was wearing was secondhand, but it was still performing its purpose of allowing me to portray myself in the way that I wanted to be regarded. He commended me for being honest and then asked if I would share the location of where I purchased this suit second hand. I immediately shared with him the address and also began to tell him the perfect time to go to this particular goodwill store to get first picks of new shipments that would come in weekly. One of the strategies that you may want to use is to find out when the major shipments of clothing comes in at a particular goodwill store. Once you find out when the shipment comes in you can then get there and have first pick over the new additions on the floor room before others get a chance to purchase them. Where I lived, Tuesday morning was the day when the new shipment of clothing would arrive at the goodwill nearest to me. I made sure that I was first in line on Tuesday mornings to go through all the new arrival of clothes and find out what great bargains that I would have the opportunity to purchase. Finally, please note that there is no shame in my game of my goodwill shopping expeditions. Even today, I still shop at goodwill stores in my neighborhood where I live. A wealthy mindset never stops saving money by purchasing goods of value at the least expense.

Reflection and Plan of Action

_____

_____

_____

_____

_____

_____

_____

_____

_____

_____

_____

_____

_____

_____

_____

Chapter 4

The Whip Appeal Principle

Here's another secret that the very wealthy live by. Very seldom will a wealthy person buy a luxury or exotic car brand new and pay cash for it. One of the things that most people don't realize is that luxury and exotic cars have a model product life cycle where nothing visibly changes on the car between 5 and 10 years. That is correct. There is a reason that luxury and exotic manufacturers have such a long product life cycle on the design of their cars. Firstly, there are only a limited number of people that will even purchase these types of vehicles because of the price. Secondly, those that purchased these vehicles will only purchase them at a set period of time which is not every other year or even two years. Therefore, what manufacturers of these types of vehicles will do is tweak the interior or the front or back lights of an automobile but everything else pretty much stays the same. The rich mindset says that it will not purchase a car brand new but will wait a year or two for it to depreciate and then make the purchase. Never forget that automobiles are some of the fastest depreciating assets that anyone can ever own. As a result, it is best to wait one, two or even more years before you purchase these types of vehicles. The average person will not know that the car is two or three years old because their mindset hasn't ever focused on how much they cost or even when they were produced. It is very easy for a rich minded person to ride in style and pay less per month for a vehicle than others do who own lesser luxurious modeled cars. Another thing to remember when it comes to buying a car, I strongly recommend to never pay cash for a luxury or exotic car. I strongly recommend to become a member of a credit union because they offer the best financial rates. Their rates are usually the best when it comes to purchasing these types of vehicles. If you buy an exotic or luxury car at a dealership and they are offering zero percent interest or a competitive rate then that would be the best route to go when it comes to financing the car. Here is another tip that a rich mindset will employ. One of the reasons to finance a car versus paying cash for it is because you then have the ability to take the lump sum of money that you were going to pay cash for the car and put it in the equity markets and let the return from the equity markets make the monthly payment on your car. Did you get that? Are you sure? Instead of taking all of your cash and paying for a car outright, take that cash money that you would have paid for the car and invest it in the equity markets and let the return each month on that lump sum of money make the monthly payment on your car. Let's look at it another way, if you can get a 10% return on your money in the equity markets and the financing on the car is 4 or 5%, you would come out on top by investing the lump sum and making the payment each month off of the return of what you have invested. Again this is a rich mindset. This is a wealthy mindset tip that I am sharing at this point. Finally, I want to share about how I know someone that bought a $235,000 exotic car and others criticized him for making such a purchase. He did not pay them any attention because what they did not know was that he was also renting out the car to local limousine companies who were paying him $1200 to $2300 per night to use the car for their most affluent clients that demanded to be chauffeured around in an exotic automobile. He would take that money and apply it towards his monthly payment! Do you now see how the rich and wealthy mindset operates? It operates on making money work for them and them not working so much for their money. You will have entered a wealthy mindset that no one can ever take away from you once you are able to take what others work hard for and turn it into something that works just as hard for you.

> *You will have entered a wealthy mindset that no one can ever take away from you once you are able to take what others work hard for and turn it into something that works just as hard for you.*

You will then prosper and sustain that prosperity the rest of your life.

Reflection and Plan of Action

_____

_____

_____

_____

_____

_____

_____

_____

_____

_____

_____

_____

_____

_____

_____

Chapter 5

The Living Legacy Principle

I t amazes me that whenever I hear someone talk about generational wealth, they are usually talking about what is transferred from them to their loved ones when they depart from this life. However, we must begin to think differently about how we transfer wealth to the next generation. We must create, establish and transfer our wealth to the next generation while we are still alive and healthy. I want to introduce the living legacy principle. The living legacy principle is simply having the ability to create, establish and sustain wealth while one is living and can watch all their beneficiaries enjoy their inheritance. It's pretty simple. One very basic idea that I strongly advocate is that people who have children who have completed high school, college, or are gainfully employed, allow them to stay at home for free. Do this instead of doing what 99% of most parents do, which is to force them to leave the house. Or require them to pay a certain monthly amount towards their room and board in the home that they've lived in ever since they were born. Again, once your child has finished high school and or college, and has obtained gainful employment, let them stay at your house three or more years free of charge. That's right! Let them stay absolutely 100% free of charge at home. Now here's the caveat. Require them to participate in their 401K, 403B or 457B plan on their job, open up a brokerage account at Charles Schwab or other reputable firms, develop a joint checking and savings account with them where you can have access to it. Afterwards, monitor their 401K, 403B and 457B participation contributions, along with their checking and savings accounts regularly. Let them know that you will allow them to live rent free for a certain number of years as long as they are not spending their money foolishly on things that are not contributing to their wealth creation. I know a family where their two children have graduated from college and are working jobs presently. Collectively the children have amassed over $100,000 in their investments, checking, and savings account In less than two years. Additionally, their parents still pay their health and their car insurance as well. Most people do not know that the law has changed and allow parents to carry children as long as they want to on their health and car insurance in many states. Also note that this family bought cars for both of their children when they were in high school and they are paid off and in good mechanical running condition. Therefore, there has been no need for them to take on additional debt by purchasing another car. Let's be honest, with rent and housing costs so high these days, it is impossible for young people to make a healthy and wealthy start in life if their living expenditures exceed their income. This is not a new principle that I am introducing here. Most European countries have utilized this strategy for centuries where even if one of the children becomes married, they will still live in the house for a number of years to accumulate wealth. Think about this principle. The living legacy principle allows you to create, establish and sustain a wealth transfer to your children while you are still living and can watch them enjoy their lives. It also brings another added benefit. It will reduce the chance of them ever coming to you for money to buy a car, house, or other things after they have obtained such a great amount of money over the years of living with you and wisely investing their money. The living legacy principle is one of the surest ways to reduce financial hardship for the next generation of your loved ones. Again, in my neighborhood I noticed this happening in the early 2000s that when students would graduate from high school or college, their parents would refurbish the basement and allow them to live rent free for years until they were able to afford a down payment on a home. This is a principle that we must begin to employ. It will change the focus and the financial fabric in our family members' lives.

Reflection and Plan of Action

_____

_____

_____

_____

_____

_____

_____

_____

_____

_____

_____

_____

_____

_____

_____

_____

Chapter 6

The 10–15–75 Principle

The 10/15/75 principle is probably the most important principle in this entire reading. It is a simple yet potent principle presented in this text. The first part of this principle teaches that 10% of your gross income should be given to the Lord at your local place of worship. This is a tough one for a lot of people. But yet is one of the greatest promises of provision that has ever been given by the Creator to establish and maintain financial wealth in our lives. This means that every pay period the very first thing that you should ever do is set aside 10% to be given to your church where you worship weekly in person or remotely. Secondly, 15% should be given to yourself. That's right! You should begin to discipline yourself to pay yourself and treat yourself as if you were a bill. Think about it for a moment, your water electric and gas bill has always been given priority by you to be paid at the proper time. Isn't it interesting to know that as you set those bills as a priority, you are always able to pay them when they are due? Now the rich mindset says that I am the most important bill that must be paid aside from giving God Yahweh 10 percent each pay period. I want to share a secret here. The secret is that when you begin to treat yourself as a bill, God Yahweh will begin to make sure you never miss a payment.

> *When you begin to treat yourself as a bill, God Yahweh will begin to make sure you never miss a payment.*

This is a beautiful thing that you should experience in your life. Once you consider yourself a bill, your creator will begin to make sure that you are able to make each payment. The message here is to simply begin to pay yourself 15% at every pay period and you will get so used to doing it that you will not miss spending it. As a bonus, you will begin to have an increase in money to spend on other things just because you made a commitment to pay yourself first and treat yourself as a bill. The final piece to the 10/15/75 principle is that now Uncle Sam will take his cut from this and you will have the rest of this discretionary portion of your income to pay bills, spend on necessities and other things. Here is also another bonus. Once you are committed to the 10% and 15% components of this principle out always, you will begin to see a miraculous increase in the remaining 75% of what you have left. If you decide to now invest more in yourself and more in your giving to the place where you worship, exponential financial increase will begin to take place in your life. You will begin to experience unexpected promotions, you will begin to experience double digit returns in your investments, you will begin to experience less unexpected emergency outlays that you used to incur. You will begin to experience the windows of heaven opening up and showering financial blessings on you to sustain your financial wealth. I know a young man who was only making a minimum wage of $4.25 an hour, and he decided to try the 10/15/75 principle. He started giving 10% to his place of worship and within a short period of time he received a promotion with an increase in pay. He then decided to go beyond giving 10% to his place of worship and he began to give 15 to 20% a year of his gross income. And yet again, he experienced a substantial increase and promotion at his place of employment. He became a supervisor where he was working and was given a company car along with yearly bonuses as well. He didn't stop there; he not only increased his giving to his church he increased his 401K contributions at his place of employment and yet he

received another promotion and an increase in his yearly bonus. There's an old adage that says you can't beat God's giving. This is a very true statement and it all hinges on you giving to God first. Giving to yourself second. Then letting God take care of the rest of the financial responsibilities in your life. It's a principle that has been tested and proven and one that you should not ever delay in implementing. Start giving so you can start getting. It's just that simple.

Reflection and Plan of Action

_____

_____

_____

_____

_____

_____

_____

_____

_____

_____

_____

_____

_____

_____

_____

Chapter 7

The Grace Period Principle

One of the best ways to create and sustain wealth is to not get caught in the credit card trap. The credit card trap is when you charge a bunch of items and not pay them off before the billing cycle occurs. Most people don't understand how the billing cycle as it pertains to credit card works. What most people do is charge a bunch of items on their credit card and instead of paying off the entire amount that they charged during that month, they pay only a portion of the total amount they charged for that billing period. This is problematic because not only do you owe what you charged, you will also be charged additional interest on what you owe. Currently, interest rate charges for credit cards are between 20% and 23%. That is a lot of money. Honestly, I believe those types of rates should be illegal. Not only do people get caught in the credit card trap of not paying their bill in full on the due date, but they also miss an important savings by not paying before the billing cycle occurs. Let me explain. Many refer to this as understanding the grace period of your credit card. The grace period is the time between the end of a billing cycle and the date your payment is due. You must check with your credit provider and find out when the billing cycle ends and the date that your payment is due. You can usually find this online. Once you figure that out, always pay during the grace period. You will not be charged any interest at all and subsequently, you will always have a very good credit score showing that you know how to manage your finances that are charged. Advice has been given to never own a credit card. However, I view that differently. For example, I use credit cards to protect me when I purchase items. For example, American Express and other credit card issuers will investigate when you have a complaint about an item that you have bought that did not live up to your expectations or was not ever received. They will begin to investigate and resolve the issue. If you had paid cash for those purchases, you probably would have found yourself losing money by not being able to get a refund. Therefore, credit cards offer many benefits in protecting you from being mistreated by certain businesses that refuse to refund or correct whatever problems you have with a purchase. Another added benefit of credit cards is that many offer perks that include discounts on flights, clothing purchases and other types of business transactions you will be involved in. Honestly, I don't use credit cards for the perks, rewards, or points that they offer. I strictly use them for the protection of my purchases in case I ever have any disputes or grievances at all. Finally, having a credit card is one of the best ways to build a great credit rating. It is strongly recommended to not have more than three credit cards. Also a tip to remember is to never charge more than 1/3 of what your total credit limit is on a credit card and not pay it off during the grace period. If you charge more than 1/3 of your credit limit on a credit card, it will negatively impact your credit score. A credit card is a great tool to have when conducting personal and business transactions. It is a great way to track records of business and other expenses. It is an excellent way to manage and protect your purchases. And it is a perfect way to protect yourself from scams and mistreatment by unethical businesses and people. Never forget to beat the billing cycle and you will beat the credit card trap.

> *Never forget to beat the billing cycle and you will beat the credit card trap.*

Reflection and Plan of Action

_____

_____

_____

_____

_____

_____

_____

_____

_____

_____

_____

_____

_____

_____

_____

_____

Chapter 8

The Ownership Principle

One of the best ways to create and sustain generational wealth is to own your own business. Owning your own business allows you to maximize your wealth because you can create services and products to meet the needs that are being unmet by others. According to Zippia, which is a small business data research firm, businesses that have between 1 to 4 employees have a net income of

$347,000 per year. That is a lot of money to contribute to the generational wealth creation for your family. Don't let anyone fool you, starting a business is a lot of hard work. You will need a lot of patience to endure the challenges that you will face. There will be a steep learning curve that will exist between you, employees, vendors, suppliers, accountants and many other entities. You will work hard. You will face disappointments and you will become tired. However, the rewards of owning your own business outweighs all of the challenges that you will incur. The secret to having a successful business is to first establish a mission, vision and value statement that will communicate your uniqueness and your willingness to provide exceptional services and products to your customers. Don't ever focus on just making money in your business. Your focus should be on creating value and quality for unmet needs that exist in the marketplace.

> *Don't ever focus on just making money in your business. Your focus should be on creating value and quality for unmet needs that exist in the marketplace.*

When quality and value creation is your main focus, the money will come exponentially to you. Another area that you must look at when you become a business owner is to make sure that you treat your employees equitably and pleasantly. If you disrespect your employees and outwardly mistreat them, it will not take long for the community that you serve to realize that you are more concerned about making money than you are about creating value for people and improving the lives of those that work for you. Owning a business requires a great deal of patience, learning and adjusting. You must be able to adapt to economic changes that will definitely occur in whatever market you are serving. You must have an attitude to be a constant learner in order to keep up with cutting edge technology and other means of how your business can serve in a very competitive marketplace. If you practice strong business and managerial principles, it will not take a long time for you to create a sustainable business that will bring you long term wealth and satisfaction in knowing that you have changed people's lives at multiple levels who come into contact with what you offer. You can have a great product or service but not offer a positive experience to customers when they encounter and engage your business and you will not be successful. It is not very difficult to do the right thing when it comes to business practices particularly in how you treat your customers and your employees. Finally, make sure you expose your children and other family members to your business at all levels in order for you to create a succession plan. One of the saddest things that I have witnessed as a consultant for many businesses is that the company is independently run by the sole proprietor. Unfortunately, when the sole owner experiences bad health or even death, the business usually closes because of a lack of a succession plan. Generational wealth says that you will always have a succession plan to not only maintain the business but allow the business to become more than it has ever been even when you were in charge of it. Start your business! Don't hesitate! Seize every opportunity! There are many opportunities in this country to own a successful business. And when you take the first step to start your business, you will begin realizing your financially and economically prosperous future.

Reflection and Plan of Action

_____

_____

_____

_____

_____

_____

_____

_____

_____

_____

_____

_____

_____

_____

_____

_____

Chapter 9

The Indexing Principle

Y ou don't have to be a financial genius to become a millionaire. You don't even need a college degree in finance to become a millionaire. You don't have to understand alpha and beta statistics to become a millionairc. One of the greatest secrets that I want to share with you to become a millionaire is to explore the principle of indexing. One of the most proven indexing vehicles is the S&P 500. Historically, since 1957 the S&P 500 has produced average annual returns of 10.13%. The S&P 500 is comprised of 500 companies that are publicly traded in the stock market. If on July 24, 2023, you had invested $600 every month since 1993 in an S&P 500 mutual fund or ETF, you would have amassed $1.3 Million dollars. Can you believe that? And if you keep doing the same thing by 2033 you will have $3.5 Million dollars. Do I have your attention yet? It is very easy to become a millionaire in America. You must have patience and discipline. Indexing is a wonderful way to become wealthy without the undue stress of the market's fluctuations that occurs with owning just one individual stock. Now let's look at some ways you can create wealth starting today. If you are 23 years old. Look below how much you will have in 10 years if you invest $600 monthly.

End Amount	Additional Contribution	Return Rate	Starting Amount	Investment Length

Starting Amount	$600		Results	
After	10 years		**End Balance**	**$122,430.80**
Return Rate	10 %		Starting Amount	$600.00
Compound	annually		Total Contributions	$72,000.00
Additional Contribution	$600		Total Interest	$49,830.80

Yes, that is $122,431 you will have at the age of 33. Now, let's see how much that will be if you keep investing $600 a month for an additional 10 years when you become 43.

End Amount	Additional Contribution	Return Rate	Starting Amount	Investment Length

Starting Amount	$600		Results	
After	20 years		**End Balance**	**$438,428.54**
Return Rate	10 %		Starting Amount	$600.00
Compound	annually		Total Contributions	$144,000.00
Additional Contribution	$600		Total Interest	$293,828.54

Look at what happens. You will have $438,429 dollars at the age of 43. How did this happen? It happened because of one of the greatest inventions on earth besides the wheel which is compound interest. So many people are victims of compound debt. The rich mindset is a producer of compound interest.

> **So many people are victims of compound debt. The rich mindset is a producer of compound interest.**

Let's go a little further. Let's say you do this for another 10 years until the age of 53. Let's see how much money you would have.

End Amount	Additional Contribution	Return Rate	Starting Amount	Investment Length

Starting Amount	$600		Results	
After	30 years		End Balance	$1,258,045.27
Return Rate	10 %		Starting Amount	$600.00
Compound	annually		Total Contributions	$216,000.00
Additional Contribution	$600		Total Interest	$1,041,445.27

Wala! You have approximately $1.3 Million dollars! And it only took you 30 years to become one. At 53 years old you are still young enough to enjoy your money with good health. Additionally, you still have many years to increase your wealth as well. Now, let's say you become aggressive in your investments at age 23 and contributed $1300 monthly for twenty years. Look at how much money you will have in 20 years.

End Amount	Additional Contribution	Return Rate	Starting Amount	Investment Length

Starting Amount	$1,300		**Results**	
After	20	years	**End Balance**	**$949,928.50**
Return Rate	10	%	Starting Amount	$1,300.00
Compound	annually		Total Contributions	$312,000.00
Additional Contribution	$1,300		Total Interest	$636,628.50

Wow! At age 43, you could consider yourself a millionaire. It's just that easy. But don't forget that it takes patience and discipline. And, if you get married each one could split that at $650 each. So, if you started investing for the first time at age 30, you would need to invest $1300 a month to become a millionaire in 20 years at age 50. I am sure you get the picture now. The longer you wait to invest, the more money you must contribute to reach the millionaire status in your lifetime.

> *The longer you wait to invest, the more money you must contribute to reach the millionaire status in your lifetime.*

All you have to do is set the age that you want to become a millionaire, establish how much you must contribute monthly and choose an S&P 500 ETF indexing fund or mutual fund and sit back, relax and watch your financial situation blossom. Ok, here is one last one just for the fun of it. Let's say you want to be a millionaire in 10 years. It doesn't matter what your age is. From the graph below, you will need to invest $5000 monthly. I will explain what ETFs and mutual funds are later in this book.

End Amount	Additional Contribution	Return Rate	Starting Amount	Investment Length

Starting Amount	$5,000	**Results**	
After	10 years	End Balance	$1,020,256.71
Return Rate	10 %	Starting Amount	$5,000.00
Compound	annually	Total Contributions	$600,000.00
Additional Contribution	$5,000	Total Interest	$415,256.71

Yes, it would only take $5000 a month for 10 years for you to become a millionaire. Does that seem impossible to you? It shouldn't. The rich mindset knows that if one was to marry and each person invests $2500 a month for 10 years, you will reach the goal easily and stress free. The rich mindset knows that if one can live at home, rent and expense free with their parents they can obtain this goal easily. This is the difference between rich mindset thinking and an impoverished mindset thinking. Which mindset do you have?

Reflection and Plan of Action

_____

_____

_____

_____

_____

_____

_____

_____

_____

_____

_____

_____

_____

_____

_____

Chapter 10

The Participation Principle

Make sure that you participate in your 401K, 403B or 457B plan that are offered at your place of employment. Begin as soon as you are eligible to participate in these programs. Interestingly, as of 2024, there are 540,000 401K millionaires in America. And even more interesting, the top five occupations that produce these millionaires are teachers, engineers, accountants, managers and lawyers. Did you notice that doctors didn't make the list? That is because doctors make a lot of money and spend more than they save. They are not very good managers of their money. Even more interestingly, teachers made the list. You may wonder, how is that possible as we know that teacher salaries are some of the lowest paying in America. Well, there are a couple of factors that contribute to their wealth. One, they save more than they spend. Two, they are great money managers and budget with great discipline and thirdly, they have one of the best 401K companies that manage their finances. That company is TIAA. TIAA offers great financial investment vehicles with very low and no cost managerial fees. Let's get into the details of the benefits of 401Ks and other retirement programs. Planning for retirement should be an important part of everyone's financial goals and security in life. Among the various retirement savings options available, 401K, 403B and 457B plans stand out due to all their great benefits for the average person. In fact, company sponsored 401K, 403B and 457B retirement plans are the number one way Americans become millionaires! These plans offer tax advantages, employer contributions, and high contribution limits. One of the best benefits of a 401K plan is that most employers offer a matching percentage based on the amount that you contribute each pay period. Your employer will offer to match a portion of your contributions, anywhere from 3% to 6%. I hope that it hasn't taken you long to see that this is free money that is given to you in your retirement savings plan. It significantly increases the amount of money that you will have when you retire. Another key benefit is that all the contributions that you make in these plans are pre-taxed. That is, the amount of your income that is taxed is reduced by the amount that you contributed in your 401K. You have to check each year to see how much you are allowed to contribute. Historically, the government increases how much you can contribute each year. For example, in 2025, the contribution limit is $23,500, with an additional catch-up contribution of $7,500 for those aged 50 and older. Also, if you are between the ages of 60-63, in 2025, you can take advantage of the higher catch-up plan which allows you to invest an additional $11,250 to the $23,500. That totals to $34,750 dollars that is pre-taxed. Think about the positive effect that has on your tax returns based on your income. My advice is to take advantage of the 401K, 403B and other retirement programs and max out on the amount that you contribute each year. Here is an example of how you will lower your taxes by participating in your 401K program. Let's say you contributed just a mere 5% of your salary in your 401K plan. Five percent of a $40,000 annual salary is $2,000 saved for the entire retirement in a year. Therefore, that $2,000 you invested is deducted as pre-tax. As a result, your total taxable income is now $38,000 instead of $40,000. Because this is in the 25% income tax bracket, you will now only have to pay Uncle Sam $9,500 in taxes versus $10,000! That is a great saving of $500 annually in tax expenses. You can't lose by participating in a 401K, 403B or 457B plan. Don't hesitate in joining these programs that are offered at your place of employment. They are some of the best ways to become a millionaire that exist in America today. Sadly, 43.5% of all Americans don't participate in companies that offer 401K and other similar programs.

Reflection and Plan of Action

_____

_____

_____

_____

_____

_____

_____

_____

_____

_____

_____

_____

_____

_____

_____

_____

Chapter 11

The Homework Principle

O ne of the most stressful experiences you will ever face is when you decide to buy an automobile. However, this text will help you significantly reduce the stress that you will experience when buying a new car. First, let's talk about the sticker price that you will see on the dealer lot. Notice that it is called the manufacturer's suggested retail price (MSRP). Please note the second word in the heading of a sticker tag that you will see on a car. It clearly states that the price is suggested. That means that they are giving you the right to negotiate a fair price with them. You should never pay sticker price for a brand-new car. I know you may want this car really bad. You might be told that it is the hottest selling car in the market right now. You may even be duped into believing that someone else had just departed and was genuinely considering purchasing this car. Rule #1, always be prepared to walk away from the deal. Rule #2, never let your emotions override judicial and prudent thinking when you are considering a purchase of a new car. Rule #3, do your homework before you ever step on the dealer lot. Preparation is the key to getting a fair deal when you are considering the purchase of a new car. First, you must know the optimal times of the month and day to purchase a car where you are more likely to get a favorable deal. The best day to purchase a car is at the end of the month. The best month to purchase a car is during December or holiday weekends. The reason that the end of the month is the optimal time to obtain a favorable deal is because dealers and salespeople are trying to reach their quotas of car sales. The end of the year is also a great time to purchase a car because dealerships are trying to reduce inventories. One of the worst times to ever consider buying a new car is during the months of September through the end of October. This is the time period when the new models have just been sent to the dealers and they are trying to maximize their profits by hyping the new styles and amenities etc. Now that you understand the optimal times to purchase a car in order to obtain a favorable deal, let's look at the intricacies of negotiating a good deal. First, do your research and obtain a dealer invoice concerning the car that you are considering. You can obtain factory invoices through popular websites like edmunds.com, consumerreports.com and other reputable automobile online publications. Once you obtain the factory invoice, you must then go through it meticulously and understand all the elements that are in it. Let's look at an example of MSRP versus Factory invoice pricing. If the sticker price (MSRP) is 32,000 for a car and you obtain the factory dealer invoice and it says, 27,500. That lets you know up front that at the very minimum you can save $4,500 on the purchase of that car. Once you have your invoice copy, walk into the dealership and ask the salesperson to show you the invoice. It should be the same as you have or very close to it. Never forget to do this. But don't stop here when negotiating this deal. There is more money to be saved. Ask the salesperson what the holdback percentage on this car is. Watch the salesperson frown and get up and go to the sales manager's desk. You are never getting a fair deal on a new car purchase unless the salesperson has to get up and get approval from the sales manager. The dealer holdback is a set amount of money that is paid back to a car dealership by the manufacturer after they sell a new car. It is a guaranteed profit margin for the dealer that the car manufacturer provides for them. It is a certain percentage of the vehicle's MSRP

(Manufacturer's Suggested Retail Price) that ranges 1% to 3%. I would calculate the 3% in my offer for the car as well. That would put you now at $26,600 versus $32,000, which was the original MSRP. That is a savings of $5400! Can you use that savings for something else? I think so. However, don't stop here. There may be more ways to save even more. Do your homework and make sure that there is not an additional factory rebate and or dealer incentive as well. You have to ask for this, because many times they don't advertise this unless they are really trying to sell cars that are not in demand. Let's say on this same car purchase you now find out that there are two other incentives on this car. This is money that the manufacturer gives the dealership so they have no problem giving it to you. They don't have a problem not giving it to you either, because they will profit from it themselves if you never ask for it. Let's say that you find out that there are two more discounts; (1) a $600 instant customer rebate and (2) a $1,000 factory to dealer incentive. That totals to $1,600

in additional savings to you. You have now negotiated a great deal for this car that saved you a total of $7000.00. You walk out the door paying only $25,000 for this brand-new car. And you got this great deal because you did your homework. Now make sure that you do the same when it comes to financing the car. Do your homework. If you belong to a credit union, I strongly recommend you start there and get an approval before you ever set foot on the dealer lot. If you don't belong to a credit union, you must join one immediately. Their financial terms are always the best you can find. However, sometimes dealers offer special low and even zero percent interest rates on cars they are motivated to sell. But make sure you check the fine print. Get a copy of all your credit score reports from the major three reporting agencies. Also, make sure you get your specific automobile credit score. It is different from your general credit score. Carry them in your hand when you go to the dealership. You may be surprised that they have a different score than you do. I remember when my

wife and I decided to refinance our home because the interest rates were at the lowest we had ever seen and we wanted to make sure that we got the best prime lending rate that was available at that time. I remember copying all three of my mortgage credit scores and when we sat down with the lender to go over the final refinancing paperwork, he gave us a score that was significantly lower than the score that we had pulled on our credit report that very morning. I remember him smiling and saying, I'm sorry, but based on your score we might not be able to give you the prime lending rate. I then proceeded to show him all three of my mortgage specific credit scores that I had pulled that morning and how they were different from his scores. He frowned, got up from his desk, walked away and came back in about 15 minutes and apologized for his mistake and gave us the prime lending rate that is reserved for those with exceptional credit. We had exceptional credit, which was well above 800 and yet we had to fight to get what we rightly deserved! Again, you must do your homework. If you don't do your homework you're going to be taken advantage of when you are doing business as you purchase things in your life. Again, when it comes to financing your automobile do your homework to make sure that you are not taken advantage of. Make sure that you get an equitable rate on your deal. Never set down and tell them how much money you want to pay per month for the car. That is one of the biggest mistakes you can ever make when negotiating your deal. Only finance based on the price of the car and the number of months you want to pay for the car. A good rule of thumb is to not finance a brand-new car for longer than 36 to 48 months. If you finance longer than that and you decide to buy another car and trade that one in, you will find yourself upside down on your loan. Being upside down means that you owe more on the car than what it is worth. Always remember that a car is a depreciating asset during a certain period of ownership. If you find yourself contemplating financing a car for more than 48 months, that is really a signal to you that you can't afford this particular car. You should not buy it at all. Another rule of thumb that I follow is to never pay a down payment on a new car. Never forget the homework principle. It will save you a lot of money and provide years of enjoyment when it comes to big purchases that you make in your lifetime.

Reflection and Plan of Action

_____

_____

_____

_____

_____

_____

_____

_____

_____

_____

_____

_____

_____

_____

_____

Chapter 12

The Credit Confident Principle

I remember not long ago how a young person shared with me how they walked into the credit union confidently with their credit report in hand and showed them their exceptional 850 perfect credit score. They told me how they then adamantly made sure that the clerk at the credit union understood that they were well qualified to get the lowest interest rate available that is reserved only for their very best customers. However, they said that they were quickly humbled as the clerk at the credit union came back with her copy of their credit report and told them that they were selling themselves short concerning what their true credit score was, because they had a FICO score of 882. They shared that they didn't understand how they could have a higher score than a perfect 850. She immediately told them that apparently they had not reviewed how credit scores are classified. She then explained to them how to correctly understand their credit score and the various classifications that exist. Take a look at the summary of the different classifications of a credit score on the next page. There are seven (7) credit score classifications. Did you know that?

GENERAL CREDIT SCORE

The General Score FICO Score 8 (300-850)

CREDIT CARDS

- Fico Bankcard Score 2 (250-900)

- Fico Bankcard Score 3 (300-850)

- Fico Bankcard Score 8 (250-900)

AUTO

- Fico Auto Score 2 (250-900)

- Fico Auto Score 8 (250-900)

MORTGAGE

Fico Score 2 (300-850)

As you can see, there are seven (7) different credit scores that you will have with Experian credit reporting service.

The first score is the general score. This is the score with which we are most familiar. It is the first one that populates when we query to find out what our overall credit score is. It is more commonly known as the general score and the fico score 8 and it has a range from a low of 300 to a maximum score of 850. Again, this is the general score. It only gives a creditor an overall broad view of how you are managing your credit. This is the score that my friend walked into the credit union with, not knowing that there are six other classification scores that existed. There's another branch of classifications of credit scores that exist and that is under the heading of credit cards. There are three different credit card scores that you will have and it's based on the different types of credit cards that you may have. The first credit card score is called the fico bankcard score 2 and it has a range from a low of 250 to a maximum high of 900. The second type of credit card score you can have is called the fico bankcard score 3 and it has a range from a low of 300 to a high and maximum of 850. The final classification of a credit card score that you will have is the fico bankcard score 8 and it has a low range of 250 and a maximum score of 900. Please note that at any time any lender can look at any one of these particular scores or all three of them and decide on what type of rate you qualify for. The next classification of credit scoring is that which deals with automobiles. Experian has two different classifications. The first classification is the auto fico score 2 and it has a range from a low of 250 to a maximum credit score of 900. The second type of auto loan credit classification score is called the fico auto score 8 and it has a minimum credit score of 250 and a maximum of 900 as well. Once again, a lender can use either one of these two or both of these two in deciding on what type of interest rate you qualify for. Finally there is the mortgage rate credit score classification. However, there is only one of those. It is labeled the fico score 2 and has a minimum score rating of 300 and a maximum of 850. Isn't it amazing how many different credit scores and classifications that exist when you are trying to buy something and a lender is trying to evaluate your creditworthiness? It is important that you stay on top of the changes that take place with how these credit scores are calculated and what the ranges are because they change all the time. Finally it's important to be credit confident to know how your credit score is calculated. Again, we are pretty much talking about the general overall credit score. Let's evaluate the illustration below.

Experian FICO SCORE 8 (General Score)

- **35% payment history**
- **30% amount of debt**
- **15% length of credit history**
- **10% amount of new credit**
- **10% credit mix**

We can see here that based on the Experian fico score 8 which is the general score that gives lenders a bird's eye view of your overall management of credit. First, thirty-

five percent of your fico score is based on your payment history. It is important that you always pay your bills on time. Next, thirty percent of your credit score is based on the amount of debt that you carry. Again, it's important that you understand how to properly utilize your credit card purchase limit amount. The general rule of thumb is to never carry a balance of more than one third of your maximum credit limit on a credit card and always pay the balance during the grace period. Fifteen percent of your credit score is based on how long you have had credit. Your credit history is very important. It is a way for a lender to determine how you handle bills and what type of debt you have incurred over time as well as your ability to pay them off. Ten percent of your credit score is based on the amount of new credit that is showing up in your report. This is a very important weight in the credit scoring algorithm as it can signal whether you are desperately trying to find money to pay bills. It can also signal that you have a cash flow management problem. Finally, ten percent of your total

FICO 8 score is based on your credit mix. This pertains to how much revolving, mortgage, auto and other types of debt that you currently have. Please know that the criteria of all credit scoring agencies changes all the time. Oh, and a general credit score of 760 will qualify you for the best interest rates from most lenders. You must do your homework in order to stay abreast of any changes that might take place. It is important to understand the seven credit classifications and constantly monitor them for any changes. A rich mindset always stays on top of credit reporting criteria.

Reflection and Plan of Action

_____

_____

_____

_____

_____

_____

_____

_____

_____

_____

_____

_____

_____

_____

_____

_____

Chapter 13

The Goal Getting Principle

One of the surest ways to make sure you are on track to becoming wealthy is to make sure that you develop a road map to your financial success. Most people talk about goal setting but very few talk about goal getting. Goal getting comes after you quantitatively state what you want to accomplish in a certain period of time and you then develop a plan of

action to make sure that you obtain those goals that you have established for yourself. After you develop a plan of action you must put that plan in motion. A road map will allow you to constantly evaluate and adjust your action plan and help you achieve your stated goals. First, let's take a look at a goal setting illustration below.

Financial Wealth Goal Setting Worksheet for 2024

<u>Goals:</u>

1. Increase my 401K portfolio by $50,000

2. Increase my Fidelity brokerage investments by $10,000

3. Maintain my checking account end of month balance at $5000

4. Maintain $0 balance on my credit cards each month

Next, let's take a look at a Goal Getting Worksheet.

Financial Goal Getting Worksheet 2024

Goal Getting Progress

1. Meet with HR representative December 25, 2023, to increase my 401K contributions by $50,000 _____ Place an X when complete

2. Go online January 4, 2024, and schedule new dollar amount to be transferred each pay period to yield $10,000 more at the end of 2024 _____ Place an X when complete

3. Check my banking account each month on the 25th day to make sure I am maintaining a $5000 ending balance to reduce account fees _____ Place an X when complete

4. January 1, 2024, go online and research each credit card that I own and find out their billing cycle and grace period in order to maintain a $0 balance each month on my credit card with no interest fee charges _____ Place an X when complete

Here you see two excellent examples of how to set goals and how to get goals. Use these two worksheets as you begin your prosperous journey in becoming wealthy.

Never forget that goal setting accomplishes nothing without goal getting.

> *Goal Setting accomplishes nothing without Goal Getting.*

Reflection and Plan of Action

_____

_____

_____

_____

_____

_____

_____

_____

_____

_____

_____

_____

_____

_____

_____

Chapter 14

The Diversification Principle

In the last 20+ years, one of the most popular investment vehicles that investors utilize to diversify or lower their financial risks are Exchange Traded Funds (ETFs). They track the performance of various indexes like the S&P 500 and other industry sectors. One of the main attractions of ETFs are the ability for an investor to trade them just like stocks. Unlike mutual funds that take longer to execute, you can trade ETFs on a stock exchange at any point during market hours. Whether you're an individual looking to invest, or a seasoned financial professional, ETFs are an easy and powerful investment option to help meet your goals. ETFs are more diverse than investing in individual stocks. Instead of buying a handful of individual stocks, investing in an ETF will give you instant exposure to a multitude of stocks. The main goal of ETFs are to match a particular index's performance, not beat it. As a result, an investor will also save money on management fees as well. Another diversified vehicle that investors utilize to diversify their portfolio is mutual funds. Mutual funds are investment products that pool together money from multiple investors. A mutual fund manager then actively manages and invests this money into a basket of different assets. This comes at a cost which is minimum if you do your homework and choose a reputable fund company. Make sure that you shop around and check the fees which can also come with what is called a load. You will want a no-load fee. A load is what the managing company will charge you upfront for just allowing them to invest your money. In other words, you lose money upfront before you are able to realize a return on your investment. Most traditional banks will charge a load to manage your mutual fund. The rich mindset investor will research and choose a reputable company with a long-term track record of delivering great returns with no load fees like, Fidelity, Vanguard, Charles Schwab and others. There are many reputable companies that manage mutual funds that carry no load fees and charge very little management fees. Take your time and do your homework. They offer a way for individual investors to access professional management and diversification without needing to buy individual securities themselves. There are several types of mutual funds, each with different investment objectives and strategies. From fixed-income funds, money market funds, equity funds, balanced funds, index funds and target date funds. Research and find which type of fund you want to invest in if you go the mutual fund route. You can utilize mutual funds in your financial portfolio through your 401K etc., brokerage firm and other ways. Again, research how you want to choose which route you take in participating in a mutual fund. Always make sure that you sign up to reinvest all dividends that your ETF or mutual fund yields.

Chapter 15

The Plodding Principle

The plodding principle means that you work and move with steady and laborious diligence. Your approach to becoming wealthy should be one that is methodical, patient and sensical. There are many people who are very hasty in trying to acquire their wealth and only end up frustrated, broke and depressed. Stay away from all get rich quick schemes. Never forget that nothing comes fast without you paying a serious penalty. That penalty could be losing your mind, peace and people that you love. Never compromise your integrity at the expense of trying to accumulate wealth. Your goal ought to be to lay your head on your pillow every night in comfort knowing that you are ethical in everything that you're doing in your wealth creation journey. Again, the key to becoming prosperous in all areas of your life lies at your ability to be patient, diligent and ethical. Notably, Proverbs chapter 21 verse 5 states that, *"Steady plodding brings prosperity; hasty speculation brings poverty."* What a powerful biblical scripture to never forget during your journey of wealth accumulation. Many people have been in a rush to get wealthy and have just ended up in a very impoverished and depressed state. Nothing in this life is worth gaining at the loss of your mind and tranquility. In fact, the Bible is full of wisdom that warns against gaining worldly possessions at the expense of losing your mind, health and strength. The key here is for you to plan your financial journey carefully and methodically. To reiterate what has been talked about in previous chapters, you must set goals and take your time and manage them. You must not hesitate to pivot and adjust during your journey. You might have to invest more than you thought you were able to. You might have to delay getting certain things that you want to have now. In academia, when we talk about giving up something we want today in order to get something better tomorrow, we term that opportunity cost. You may have to give up a lot of conveniences and luxuries at the start of your financial journey. But remember that it's just a temporary sacrifice that will yield a long-term prosperous future for you. One of the key principles that steady plodding consists of is learning how to live below your means without sacrificing your quality of life. You must learn how to make value purchases. That is, quality goods that will last a very long time while providing the needed utility to improve your life. Never forget that you don't have to spend the most to get the best.

> ***You don't have to spend the most to get the best.***

You must learn how to become an informed shopper who can save money without sacrificing quality. Start shopping at farmers markets for your food. Shop at various outlets for other goods. Shop at big box outlets like Costco and Sam's Warehouse for everyday items that will allow you to save tons of money. Buy your cars from auction houses. Attend city courthouse tax auctions and you might just get a house for a minimum amount of money. As stated earlier, shop at goodwill stores in affluent neighborhoods. Buy cars that are three to five years old. And when you buy those cars, make sure that you negotiate a great finance deal. Also, you should only consider paying cash for a car if it only involves three to four thousand dollars And it is in great mechanical and aesthetic shape. You should also consider buying exquisite clothes at consignment shops. You can find these easily in your community. Antique furniture stores are excellent places to begin to furnish your home.

Finally, make sure that you subscribe to Consumer Reports and various online websites that offer appliance and other product reviews and recommendations. The rich mindset has no problem plodding and being diligent as it acquires sustainable wealth without losing any peace or joy in life.

Reflection and Plan of Action

_____

_____

_____

_____

_____

_____

_____

_____

_____

_____

_____

_____

_____

_____

_____

Chapter 16

The Club Building Principle

I highly recommend joining or starting an investment club that requires no investment of money at all. The greatest benefit of joining an investment club is to learn about the stock market and the various investment opportunities that exist. Join or start an investment club that meets monthly where individuals will come together and share individual stock and other investment information with each other. You can even create a simulated stock market game where each member can compete with each other to see how their individual investment choices are doing against other members in the club. You may be wondering why I recommend a wealth investment club that doesn't require any money or exchange of money. Historically it has been very difficult to successfully operate a wealth building club that requires a financial investment by its members. A perfect example is of the Beardstown ladies who became very popular in 1995 when they boasted that they had beat the major indexes' annual returns by achieving a 23.4% return annually for many years. They even published a book that sold well over 1,000,000 copies outlining their strategies of how they obtained those great returns. However an investment firm audited their reports and found out that there were major miscalculations in their actual annual returns. They also included membership fees as a part of their investment returns. After the audit, it was stated that they only achieved 9.1% annual returns historically. There are a lot of drawbacks when establishing a wealth building club that requires a financial investment as well. Often, once members acquire a certain amount of money or a personal stake in the club, they begin to withdraw their money which hurts the overall financial position of the club. There have also been numerous reports of mismanagement of funds as well. This is why I recommend that if you decide to become a part of a club or start a club, make sure that the number one objective is to learn about the equity markets and other investment vehicles without any financial contributions involved. A designated time to hold meetings should be established. Each member should specialize in a certain sector of investments. Each member should be required to do their homework and share their thoughts and expertise at each meeting. And again, the club should set up a stock simulation game where each member can track their decisions and see how they fare against other members in the club. Investment clubs have been around for many years. However, they are not as popular as they used to be as technology has allowed individual investors to be educated and become more comfortable with the equity markets. The rich mindset is always learning and does not hesitate to increase its knowledge of how to become wealthy and sustain financial independence.

Reflection and Plan of Action

_____

_____

_____

_____

_____

_____

_____

_____

_____

_____

_____

_____

_____

_____

_____

Chapter 17

The Testate-Estate Principle

One of the saddest experiences a family can ever have is to lose a loved one and that loved one not having a will outlining how their possessions should be distributed. Sadly, 67% of people that die in America will die without having a will. This creates a very serious financial burden on family members. It creates unnecessary stress as well on how to handle their deceased loved one's final expenses. It also creates uncertainty on how to handle any outstanding debt that may exist. Also, it creates total chaos on how to divide remaining assets equitably among loved ones. It is important to make sure that you have a very concise and precise will that clearly communicates how your assets should be distributed upon your departure from this life. I would like to also stress that it is important that you review the documentation of your will with all loved ones while you are still alive. This may seem a little odd and it might seem uncomfortable to you, but it is important that everyone knows exactly how you wish your assets to be distributed and more importantly, who will be in charge over your last requests. Years ago one of the main barriers to establishing a will was the cost that lawyers would charge. However today, there are many online last will and testament programs that will allow you to correctly and succinctly craft a last will and testament that will be valid in whatever state you live in. The cost for such online will development applications range from a price of fifty to a couple of hundred dollars. They are very straightforward and simple to follow to complete. Many of these online will and last testament applications will also provide state specific rules and laws that have already been built into a template for you to navigate. Here is a list of the best online will maker platforms.

LegalZoom, Rocket Lawyer

Quicken WillMaker, U.S. Legal Wills

Total Legal, Law Depot

Nolo

Gentreo

LegalShield

LegalWills

FreeWill

Fabric by Gerber Life

When you name your executor who will be responsible for the administration of your last will and testament, make sure that it is someone that is trustworthy, wise, fair, patient, loving, stable and has your best interest at heart in the distribution of your assets. I cannot stress how important it is while you are still living to let everyone know who the designated and assigned executor is. The reason for this is very simple. Whatever animosity or misunderstanding that may exist can be expressed and explained while you are still alive. It will reduce a lot of headaches and arguments when you depart this life. Once you and your loved ones have reviewed your will while you are still living, make sure that you let everyone know where it is being placed so that it can be easily found when you die. I strongly recommend buying a very small safe to go in your house and provide the code and or keys to certain family members so that it is accessible at your point of departure from this life. And one last thing, I strongly urge you to outline in your will how much you want spent on your Funeral arrangements. Sadly, there are many people who die and the family divides up all the assets and will not contribute any of the money left to them to cover the expenses of the funeral for the dearly departed. This is sad, but very true. The rich mindset not only has a will but discusses the will with their loved ones while they are alive.

Reflection and Plan of Action

_____

_____

_____

_____

_____

_____

_____

_____

_____

_____

_____

_____

_____

_____

_____

_____

Chapter 18

The Barter Principle

I t has been reported that in the late 1800s to early 1900s that African Americans per capita were more wealthy than we are today. You may be asking yourself; how could that be? Well it's pretty simple. Mainstream America did not want to conduct business with us. They would not allow us to purchase certain things. Moreover, they would not allow us to finance anything. Therefore, we were forced to create our own economic structure. The very first thing that we did was implement a unique and powerful bartering system. For example, even up to the mid-1960s, we would build our homes and move into them debt free. You may even be asking yourself how that could be? That too is very simple. In our neighborhoods we had various skilled labor individuals that were willing to exchange their services among each other free of charge. This is what would happen when it came to building a house that was completed debt free. Someone who was a brick mason would ask a carpenter to come and frame his home and then in return he would provide all the brickwork for his house free of charge. Likewise the plumber would get with the carpenter and the brick mason and they would all exchange their services free of charge. They would continue to do this amongst each other until one of the individual's home was completed. Once they finished one person's home then they would begin to work on the next person's home and it went on until everyone had their homes-built debt free. You may even be asking yourself; how did we lose that? Why aren't we building homes for each other debt free now? Well the answer to this is very simple as well. The majority opened up their commerce to us when they realized how much we could contribute to the economic production of goods and services in America. They also realized that we had amassed a significant amount of savings because we were paying for everything that we owned and not owing anything to anyone. History has hidden the fact that African Americans owned some of the most successful banks in America in the 1800s and early 1900s. In fact, our banks were so well run that they pulled from our talent and hired us to help streamline their business practices. We allowed our talents in skills to be taken from us and given to those who didn't care about us.

> *We allowed our talents in skills to be taken from us and given to those who didn't care about us.*

As a result, we stopped adding to our economic success and contributing to other people's success at our expense. We started relying on others for our pay, not realizing that we could be more successful creating our own wealth through business ownership. From the late 1800s to early 1900s we owned more businesses than we do now per capita. We have always been entrepreneurs and skilled laborers. What we have lost is self-awareness of who we truly are and all that we can do independent of other races. The rich mindset is always looking to exchange wisdom, knowledge, skills and other assets with like-minded individuals. It is time for us to build within our communities an economic structure that no one can infiltrate and weaken as we soar to a level of wealth like we have never seen before.

Reflection and Plan of Action

_____

_____

_____

_____

_____

_____

_____

_____

_____

_____

_____

_____

_____

_____

_____

_____

Chapter 19

The Gap Closing Principle

I will now introduce "The Gap Closing Principle." The Gap Closing Principle says that there are things that we must do to reduce and possibly eradicate the huge chasm that exists between African Americans' wealth versus other races. One of the most common ways of accumulating wealth is through home ownership. Historically African Americans were deprived of home ownership after fighting in major world wars as we were not allowed to apply for VA and other loans afterwards. To make things worse, in addition to not being able to secure a loan to buy a home, The United States government red lined places where we were confined to live. White military veterans began to buy more than one home. They then turned around and rented those homes to African Americans. As a result, White Americans built their wealth by renting homes to us in massive numbers. Homeownership is one of the first ways that wealth is created in America. Let's examine the chart below. Notice that as of October 2024, 74.4% of White Americans are homeowners. 62.7% of Asian Pacific Islanders and Native Hawaiians are homeowners. 48.8% of Hispanic Americans are homeowners. However, only 46.4% of African Americans are homeowners. As you can see from the early days of being denied loans to obtain a home, we are still suffering to this very day when it comes to homeownership.

Homeownership Rate by Race

Homeownership Rate by Race

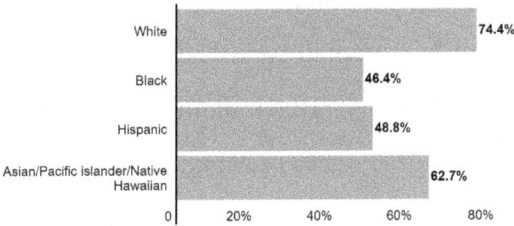

Race	Rate
White	74.4%
Black	46.4%
Hispanic	48.8%
Asian/Pacific islander/Native Hawaiian	62.7%

Source: U.S. Census Bureau, Quarterly Residential Vacancies and Homeownership, Fourth Quarter 2024, Feb. 5, 2025

Now let's look at the median wealth of all races in America.

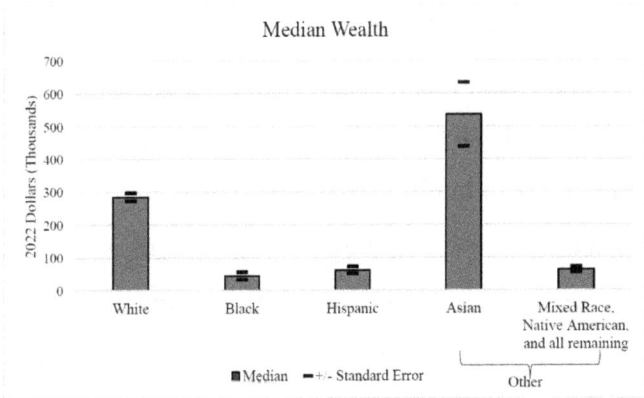

Median Wealth

According to the 2024 Board of Governors of the Federal Reserve Systems shown above, White American families had a median net worth in the amount of $285,000 whereas the net worth of the typical Black family was only $44,900, which is only about 15.8% of a White family's median wealth. That is a huge gap in wealth! Additionally, Black families had the lowest median wealth of all races in America. Hispanic families held only 21.6 percent of the wealth of the typical White family which is approximately $61,600. The remaining families, those identifying as American Indian, Alaska Native, Native Hawaiian, Pacific Islander, other race, and all respondents reporting more than one racial identification, had a median wealth slightly greater than the Black and Hispanic family, rather than the typical White or Asian family. Here is a notable statistic. Asian Americans have the highest median wealth in America at an astounding $536,000! This means that White Americans' wealth is only 53.17% of Asian Americans. That's something to ruminate on. We have a lot of work to do to close the median wealth gap in America! Let's now look at median income by race from 2019 to 2022 according to the Board of Governors of the Federal Reserve System (2023).

	Median		
	2019	2022	Percent Change
White	80.0	81.1	1.3
Black	46.7	46.0	-1.6
Hispanic	47.2	46.7	-1.1
Other	64.6	68.3	5.7

Notes: Thousands of 2022 dollars.

Source: Board of Governors of the Federal Reserve System (2023).

Notice that African Americans median income ($46,700) decreased by 1.6% from 2019 to 2022 but yet was only 57.58% of White Americans' income ($81,100)! This is staggering news to say the least. We are working the same as others but make much less. Now let's examine credit card ownership and payment statistics of all races in America according to the federal reserve (2024).

Race/ethnicity	Has a credit card	Carried a balance (among credit card holders)
Asian	90%	24%
White	86%	42%
Hispanic	74%	59%
Black	70%	72%

As you can see, Asian Americans own more credit cards than any other race. However, they are the least to carry a balance on their cards. African Americans are the least credit card owners but carry a balance more than any other racial consumer. This means that it is harder for us to get a card but once we get it we don't capitalize on saving money by paying off the amount we charge during the grace period before it is due with interest charges included in the monthly bill. Finally, let's look at investment statistics of White versus African Americans.

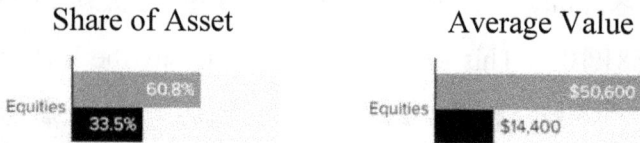

Share of Asset	Average Value
Equities 60.8% / 33.5%	Equities $50,600 / $14,400

Source: Federal Reserve Board, 2019 Survey of Consumer Finances

We can see above that African Americans only own 34% of equities whereas White Americans own 61% of equities in their financial accounts. Even more, of the 34% equity assets owned by African Americans, they only have an average of $14,000 in total investments.

Whereas, White Americans have an average asset value of $50,600. That is an astounding 261% more than what African Americans have in their investments. Now let's look at ways to reduce and possibly eradicate the wealth gap that exists among African Americans and other races in America.

Stop Playing The Lottery

The Lottery Advertising Association for Consumer Research or Cash 3, reports that 63.9% of African Americans have the highest rate of playing the lottery, significantly surpassing both Hispanics (43.8 percent) and Whites (41.2 percent). Let's say that someone spends $35 a week on lottery tickets. At the end of the year that is $1,680. However, they never win anything which is a very realistic observation. If they had put that $35 a week into an S&P 500 ETF, they would have $1909.68 at the end of the year. They would have made $229.68. Doesn't sound like a lot does it? What happens if they do that for 5 years?

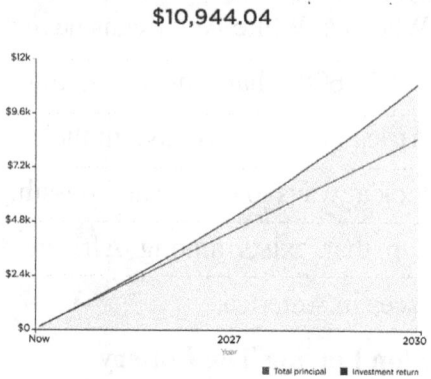

$10,944.04

Investment details

Initial investment
$140

Years of investment growth
5 Years

Estimated rate of return
10%

Compound frequency
Annually

Amount of recurring investments
$140

Recurring investment frequency
Monthly | Annually

■ Total principal ■ Investment return

If they kept investing $35 a week for 5 years, they would have $10,944.04. Regrettably, however, they have been playing the lottery for 5 years and haven't won one red cent. We must learn how to put our money in the right place. I know someone who has religiously placed $35 a week in the lottery for 20 years and have never won anything. Look at the next page at what they would have now if they only invested it in the market. Yes! They would have $101,498. Here is the exciting part. They would have only invested $33,600! Now that's the beauty and power of compound interest. Oh by the way, they asked me to lend them $140.00 not long ago to help them pay their electric bill.

$101,498.14

Investment details

Initial investment

$140

Years of investment growth

20   Years

Estimated rate of return

10%

Compound frequency

Annually

Amount of recurring investments

$140

Recurring investment frequency

| Monthly | Annually |

Chart axis labels: $110k, $89k, $67k, $45k, $22k, $0 · Now, 2035, 2045 · Year

■ Total principal ■ Investment return

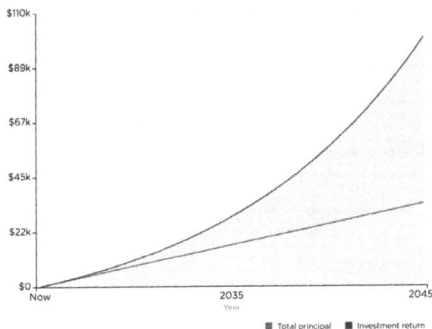

Manage Our Credit Card Debt

We must begin to research all of our credit cards and find out the billing cycle and pay off each card during the grace period in order to save interest charges. We must never charge and carry a balance of more than 1/3 of our borrowing limit on each of the credit cards that we own. We should never have more than three credit cards. And an American Express card is one of the best cards to have in our portfolio of charge cards.

We Must Get a Degree of Higher Learning

Education Level	Estimated Lifetime Earnings (millions)
Less than High School	\$1.2
High School Diploma	\$1.6
Some College, No Degree	\$1.9
Associate's Degree	\$2.3
Bachelor's Degree	\$2.8
Master's or Higher	\$3.6

There is a huge lifetime earnings difference for people who have advanced degrees. If you get a master's or higher-level degree, you can earn 200% more money in your lifetime than if you never completed high school. It doesn't matter what your age is. Begin the process of getting a higher level of education and enjoy a higher level of life.

> *Get a higher level of education and enjoy a higher level of life.*

Home Ownership

We must actively monitor our credit ratings through the major three credit reporting agencies. We must then do our homework and set goals to purchase a home. Homeownership is one of the most basic ways to begin to create wealth for a family. Currently interest rates are very high but they should soon go down and allow us to purchase homes at feasible interest rates.

Equity Markets

Finally, we must begin to invest in the equity markets. We must begin to educate ourselves in all areas of stocks, bonds, treasury bills, ETFs, mutual funds, certificate of deposits, annuities, IRAs and the many other investment vehicles that exist. It is imperative that we participate in our companies 401K, 403B or 457B retirement investment plans. When we begin to make these kinds of changes in the way we view wealth creation, we will reduce and close the wealth gap that we are now witnessing in America. The rich mindset is always learning new ways to create, sustain and transfer wealth. What are you waiting for? It is time to think rich, act rich, and get rich!

Reflection and Plan of Action

_____

_____

_____

_____

_____

_____

_____

_____

_____

_____

_____

_____

_____

_____

_____

BONUS SECTION:

BIBLICAL

INSPIRATION

FOR WEALTH

CREATION

Chapter 20

Get Busy, Get Rich

**⁴ A slack hand causes poverty,
but the hand of the diligent makes rich.**

Proverbs 10:4

The best way to prosper financially and in other areas of your life is to simply get busy. You must develop a mindset along with a work ethic to reach your financial and other prosperous goals. You must create movement through acting on what you want to achieve. Many people plan what they want, but it's the doing that makes a plan become a reality.

> *Many people plan what they want, but it's the doing that makes a plan become a reality.*

Getting started and not stopping until you have achieved your goal for prosperity should be your mantra. Don't let anything, anyone or any challenging circumstance delay or stop your progress from manifesting. The key to achieving your goal of prosperity is simply to be diligent. A diligent individual is defined as a person who is characterized by care and perseverance in carrying out tasks. This means that you not only want to achieve your goal. You are fastidious and detailed during the entire process. You will take pride in every aspect of your own business. A diligent person also displays a persevering attitude. In other words, you are persistent in all you do regardless of the difficulties or delays outside of your control. For example, you may want to start a business. You then go to the bank to request a loan, only to be turned down. This is where your diligence must be displayed. You don't give up. You go to four additional banks and they all turn you down as well. You then decide that a bank loan might not be the best place for you to obtain the financial funding you need to start your business. You then go to conferences and talk to investors and tell them about your business plans and all of them are not interested, but you still give each one your business plan and contact information. One day you get a call from one of the investors that you met. They invite you to lunch to discuss your business plan in detail. After three or four meetings, they offer you the funding you need to start your business. You look back and realize that you began this business idea three years earlier but never stopped working your plan by meeting people and telling them about what made your business special and primed to be successful. That is what being diligent is. It is about never giving up when others can't see what you believe about your plan. You must remember that the vision that God Yahweh gave you, is just that, a vision that only you can see. It is your responsibility to share your vision that is spiritual in a way that others can see it as you do. You may have to work two jobs while you wait for your vision to become a reality! You may have to sacrifice driving a new car now in order to wait on your vision to become a reality! You might have to delay wearing expensive clothes for a while, as you wait for your vision to become a reality! All of this is what being diligent entails. Look closely at Proverbs 10:4. It shows us that, *"the hand,"* makes rich. Notice it doesn't say that the hand makes one rich. In other words, the hand is the means for anyone that is willing to work to achieve a status in this lifetime of acquiring wealth. Your hand is capable of converting potential into reality.

> ***Your hand is capable of converting potential into reality.***

Your hand has the power to change things that are spiritual into things that are material. How does this happen? It happens simply by the blessing of touch. That's right! When we touch something, we do more than just place our hand on it. When we touch something, there is an anointing that God Yahweh placed in us that is released and begins to manifest right in front of our eyes. Our God given vision must become flesh in order to dwell among us.

> *Our God given vision must become flesh in order to dwell among us.*

The touching and working of your hand are what transform dreams and visions into a living and useful reality. Never forget that in the beginning of this world, God Yahweh said and things happened. However, when it came to man, God Yahweh said let us make man into our image. He then formed man out of the dust with His hand and he came into existence. Notice that the scripture clearly says that when God Yahweh formed man with His hand, he merely existed. He still wasn't alive. Only after God Yahweh breathed into his nostrils did he become a living being. Never forget that your plan for prosperity requires that you speak it, work it and give it life.

> *Never forget that your plan for prosperity requires that you speak it, work it and give it life.*

When you are given a vision, write and then tell the right people about it! Next, work your vision by releasing the

156

creative anointing that God Yahweh placed in your hand. Finally, as you are working on your plan, the breath that it takes for you to achieve each milestone of your plan will bring to life your pursuit of prosperity. Go for it! Speak it! Work it! Breathe on it! Watch your life change for the better! Prosper like you never have before! Prosper as God Yahweh wants you to! Prosper to contribute to society and those closest to you!

Reflection

Write below what you feel in your heart God is saying to you concerning the vision He has shown you about His plan for prosperity in your life.

_____
_____
_____
_____
_____
_____
_____
_____
_____
_____
_____
_____
_____
_____
_____
_____
_____
_____

Chapter 21

When You Give God Your Best, You'll Get His Better

**⁹ Honor the LORD with your wealth
and with the firstfruits of all your produce; ¹⁰ then
your barns will be filled with plenty,
and your vats will be bursting with wine.**

Proverbs 3:9-10

One of the most straightforward formulas to always prosper in all areas of your life, is to give God Yahweh your absolute best at all times! God Yahweh expects to receive the firstfruits of everything that we have. Firstfruits is an Aramaic and Hebrew term that means, the very first and best of whatever you are given. Let's look at this a little deeper. Firstfruits means that we give to God Yahweh back the absolute best of everything he has ever given us. It means it is top of mind for us. That means when we give to God Yahweh, it is not an afterthought or what we do after we have done other things with our money, time and skill set. It means that the very first thing we do is give a minimum of ten percent of all of our income immediately whenever we get paid or receive money. It means that we take pride and joy knowing that before we pay a bill, buy something or invest our money, we give God Yahweh ten percent of all of our money upfront without hesitation or any contingency. This is one of the biggest barriers most people experience when it comes to prospering in all areas of their lives. Many people say that they honor God. However, true honoring of God Yahweh involves giving back to Him a minimum of ten percent off the top of all our earnings and financial increase in life. Most people miss the promise in scripture that comes with us honoring God Yahweh with our firstfruits. The promise from God is that He will fill us with more financial resources than we can store or ever need to use in our life. Take note that this overflow of blessings is not limited to financial resources. It means that there is an overflow of health, peace, joy, success and fulfillment in all areas of our lives as well. Prosperity is more than financial gain. Prosperity means that we have a fulfilled and satisfied life in all areas of our life! It also means that money by itself doesn't bring us joy. It means that the wholeness of a meaningful life is constantly before us. We are always in a state of blissfulness that can't be shaken by any outside negative event that we may experience. It means that once we develop a mindset of giving God Yahweh our firstfruits, we will experience an overflow of prosperity in all aspects of our being. We will experience an overflow in joy, peace, love, forgiveness, hope, healing, confidence, ingenuity and excellent health. This overflow of prosperity shall never end and only flow stronger as we navigate the unending ebullience of our everyday life in the presence of God Yahweh! All that is required of us to put in motion this unending prosperous flow from

God in all areas of our lives, is to give upfront and foremost, ten percent of all our financial increase. We must also not overlook how we present firstfruits in other areas of our lives as well. For example, we should have a firstfruits mentality when it comes to our place of employment. We must have a mindset and work ethic to do and give our best at our place of employment. We should not work just to get a check. We should check to make sure that we are giving our best each and every day on our job.

> *We should not work just to get a check. We should check to make sure that we are giving our best each and every day on our job.*

We shouldn't be told what we should do in order to provide a better service to whomever we are working for. We should always think creatively about what we can do to make things better for who we have been called to serve. When we develop this mindset, we are setting ourselves up for the overflow of blessings in our lives. Are you ready to become rich? Are you ready to experience unending joy? Are you ready to walk in better health? Well then, begin to present your firstfruits in all areas of your life to God Yahweh. His words are true and powerful and will transform us into prosperous beings that others will look at and want to emulate. It's time to let your light shine. Shine your light in the dark places of others! Shine your light in the dark spaces of others' hearts! Shine your light in the dark places of people that have lost hope and have no vision of living a better life. Shine! Shine! Shine! as you reflect The Divine!

Reflection

Write below what you feel in your heart God is saying to you concerning giving and the blessing that comes from doing so.

_____

_____

_____

_____

_____

_____

_____

_____

_____

_____

_____

_____

_____

Appendices

Dow 30 Companies

Rank	Company Name	Symbol	Weight
1	Goldman Sachs Group Inc	GS	8.02948
2	United health Group Inc	UNH	7.049736
3	Microsoft Corp	MSFT	5.642744
4	Home Depot Inc	HD	5.405878
5	Sherwin Williams Co	SHW	5.216787
6	Caterpillar Inc	CAT	5.025688
7	Visa Inc Class A Shares	V	4.954241
8	Amgen Inc	AMGN	4.660705
9	McDonalds S Corp	MCD	4.609487
10	Salesforce Inc	CRM	4.058569
11	American Express Co	AXP	3.919692
12	Intl Business Machines Corp	IBM	3.752265
13	Travelers Cos Inc	TRV	3.682109

14	JPMorgan Chase & Co	JPM	3.475945
15	Apple Inc	AAPL	3.429892
16	Honeywell International Inc	HON	3.077678
17	Amazon.com Inc	AMZN	2.858602
18	Procter & Gamble Co	PG	2.524321
19	Johnson & Johnson	JNJ	2.39147
20	Chevron Corp	CVX	2.24298
21	Boeing Co	BA	2.211991
22	3m Co	MMM	2.098938
23	Nvidia Corp	NVDA	1.616742
24	Walt Disney Co	DIS	1.513732
25	Merck & Co. Inc.	MRK	1.357926
26	Walmart Inc	WMT	1.31589
27	Nike Inc Cl B	NKE	1.127516
28	Coca Cola Co	KO	1.024793
29	Cisco Systems Inc	CSCO	0.917335
30	Verizon Communications Inc	VZ	0.660814

Top 50 S&P 500 Companies

1	Apple Inc.	AAPL	7.38%
2	Microsoft Corp	MSFT	5.97%
3	Nvidia Corp	NVDA	5.64%
4	Amazon.com Inc	AMZN	3.81%
5	Meta Platforms, Inc. Class A	META	2.78%
6	Alphabet Inc. Class A	GOOGL	2.07%
7	Broadcom Inc.	AVGO	1.86%
8	Berkshire Hathaway Class B	BRK.B	1.85%
9	Alphabet Inc. Class C	GOOG	1.71%
10	Tesla, Inc.	TSLA	1.50%
11	Eli Lilly & Co.	LLY	1.40%
12	JPMorgan Chase & Co.	JPM	1.39%
13	Visa Inc.	V	1.22%
14	Exxon Mobil Corporation	XOM	0.98%
15	UnitedHealth Group Incorporated	UNH	0.92%
16	Mastercard Incorporated	MA	0.91%

17	Costco Wholesale Corp	COST	0.87%
18	Procter & Gamble Company	PG	0.85%
19	Johnson & Johnson	JNJ	0.82%
20	Walmart Inc.	WMT	0.81%
21	Netflix Inc	NFLX	0.78%
22	Abbvie Inc.	ABBV	0.77%
23	Home Depot, Inc.	HD	0.76%
24	Coca-Cola Company	KO	0.57%
25	Bank of America Corporation	BAC	0.56%
26	Salesforce, Inc.	CRM	0.55%
27	Chevron Corporation	CVX	0.53%
28	Cisco Systems, Inc.	CSCO	0.52%
29	Oracle Corp	ORCL	0.51%
30	International Business Machines Corporation	IBM	0.49%
31	Merck & Co., Inc.	MRK	0.49%
32	Abbott Laboratories	ABT	0.49%
33	Wells Fargo & Co.	WFC	0.48%
34	Philip Morris International Inc.	PM	0.48%
35	Mcdonald's Corporation	MCD	0.47%

36	Linde Plc	LIN	0.46%
37	Accenture Plc	ACN	0.44%
38	Pepsico, Inc.	PEP	0.43%
39	Ge Aerospace	GE	0.43%
40	Thermo Fisher Scientific, Inc.	TMO	0.42%
41	Adobe Inc.	ADBE	0.40%
42	At&t Inc.	T	0.40%
43	Verizon Communications	VZ	0.40%
44	The Walt Disney Company	DIS	0.39%
45	Intuitive Surgical Inc.	ISRG	0.38%
46	Qualcomm Inc	QCOM	0.37%
47	Goldman Sachs Group Inc.	GS	0.36%
48	Servicenow, Inc.	NOW	0.36%
49	Amgen Inc	AMGN	0.36%
50	Palantir Technologies Inc. Class A	PLTR	0.36%

The Top 6 NASDAQ ETFs

ETF	EXPENSE RATIO
Invesco QQQ Trust (ticker: QQQ)	0.2%
Invesco Nasdaq 100 ETF (QQQM)	0.15%
Direxion Nasdaq-100 Equal Weighted ETF (QQQE)	0.35%
Invesco ESG Nasdaq 100 ETF (QQMG)	0.2%
ProShares Ultra QQQ (QLD)	0.95%
ProShares UltraPro QQQ (TQQQ)	0.88%

Top ETFs by Assets

Symbol	Name	Asset Under Mgt
SPY	SPDR S&P 500 ETF Trust	$619,623,000.00
VOO	Vanguard S&P 500 ETF	$612,126,000.00
IVV	iShares Core S&P 500 ETF	$582,941,000.00
VTI	Vanguard Total Stock Market ETF	$459,700,000.00
QQQ	Invesco QQQ Trust Series I	$317,412,000.00
VUG	Vanguard Growth ETF	$152,856,000.00
VEA	Vanguard FTSE	$147,621,000.00

	Developed Markets ETF	
VTV	Vanguard Value ETF	$134,647,000.00
IEFA	iShares Core MSCI EAFE ETF	$130,769,000.00
BND	Vanguard Total Bond Market ETF	$126,721,000.00
AGG	iShares Core U.S. Aggregate Bond ETF	$124,631,000.00
IWF	iShares Russell 1000 Growth ETF	$101,137,000.00
IJH	iShares Core S&P Mid-Cap ETF	$91,965,400.00
VIG	Vanguard Dividend Appreciation ETF	$88,607,200.00

GLD	SPDR Gold Shares	$84,140,300.00
IEMG	iShares Core MSCI Emerging Markets ETF	$84,062,400.00
VXUS	Vanguard Total International Stock ETF	$83,237,100.00
VWO	Vanguard FTSE Emerging Markets ETF	$83,013,000.00
IJR	iShares Core S&P Small-Cap ETF	$81,816,700.00
VGT	Vanguard Information Technology ETF	$81,563,500.00
RSP	Invesco S&P 500® Equal Weight ETF	$74,732,700.00
VO	Vanguard Mid-Cap ETF	$74,169,000.00

SCHD	Schwab US Dividend Equity ETF	$69,398,100.00
XLK	Technology Select Sector SPDR Fund	$68,948,100.00
IWM	iShares Russell 2000 ETF	$65,414,900.00
ITOT	iShares Core S&P Total U.S. Stock Market ETF	$63,997,000.00
BNDX	Vanguard Total International Bond ETF	$62,580,200.00
VB	Vanguard Small Cap ETF	$61,697,500.00
IWD	iShares Russell 1000 Value ETF	$61,359,700.00
VYM	Vanguard High Dividend Yield Index ETF	$60,114,600.00

EFA	iShares MSCI EAFE ETF	$59,280,100.00
SPLG	SPDR Portfolio S&P 500 ETF	$57,543,000.00
IVW	iShares S&P 500 Growth ETF	$54,752,600.00
XLF	Financial Select Sector SPDR Fund	$52,249,700.00
SCHX	Schwab U.S. Large-Cap ETF	$51,822,700.00
IBIT	iShares Bitcoin Trust ETF	$51,597,700.00
QUAL	iShares MSCI USA Quality Factor ETF	$51,154,000.00
VCIT	Vanguard Intermediate-Term Corporate Bond ETF	$50,116,100.00

TLT	iShares 20+ Year Treasury Bond ETF	$49,780,900.00
SCHF	Schwab International Equity ETF	$43,843,600.00
VT	Vanguard Total World Stock ETF	$42,356,500.00
QQQM	Invesco NASDAQ 100 ETF	$41,927,600.00
IXUS	iShares Core MSCI Total International Stock ETF	$40,861,800.00
VEU	Vanguard FTSE All-World ex-US Index Fund	$40,841,900.00
MUB	iShares National Muni Bond ETF	$40,591,100.00
VV	Vanguard Large Cap ETF	$40,589,300.00

JEPI	JPMorgan Equity Premium Income Fund	$39,809,200.00
XLV	Health Care Select Sector SPDR Fund	$39,478,400.00
BIL	SPDR Bloomberg 1-3 Month T-Bill ETF	$39,219,000.00
IAU	iShares Gold Trust	$39,135,900.00
IWR	iShares Russell Midcap ETF	$38,428,100.00
IWB	iShares Russell 1000 ETF	$38,370,600.00
DIA	SPDR Dow Jones Industrial Average ETF Trust	$38,103,600.00
IVE	iShares S&P 500 Value ETF	$37,543,900.00

MBB	iShares MBS ETF	$37,310,700.00
SCHG	Schwab U.S. Large-Cap Growth ETF	$37,171,600.00
SGOV	iShares 0-3 Month Treasury Bond ETF	$36,380,600.00
VNQ	Vanguard Real Estate ETF	$36,298,500.00
VTEB	Vanguard Tax-Exempt Bond ETF	$36,281,500.00
VCSH	Vanguard Short-Term Corporate Bond ETF	$34,856,000.00
SPYG	SPDR Portfolio S&P 500 Growth ETF	$33,556,700.00
BSV	Vanguard Short-Term Bond ETF	$33,480,800.00

IEF	iShares 7-10 Year Treasury Bond ETF	$32,945,100.00
IUSB	iShares Core Total USD Bond Market ETF	$32,853,000.00
DFAC	Dimensional U.S. Core Equity 2 ETF	$32,617,400.00
SCHB	Schwab U.S. Broad Market ETF	$32,258,500.00
VGIT	Vanguard Intermediate-Term Treasury ETF	$31,948,400.00
LQD	iShares iBoxx $ Investment Grade Corporate Bond ETF	$31,687,900.00
JPST	JPMorgan Ultra-Short Income ETF	$30,896,300.00

DGRO	iShares Core Dividend Growth ETF	$30,889,500.00
XLE	Energy Select Sector SPDR Fund	$30,822,700.00
GOVT	iShares U.S. Treasury Bond ETF	$30,046,500.00
VBR	Vanguard Small Cap Value ETF	$29,957,000.00
VONG	Vanguard Russell 1000 Growth ETF	$25,389,900.00
SPYV	SPDR Portfolio S&P 500 Value ETF	$25,377,700.00
MGK	Vanguard Mega Cap Growth ETF	$24,414,800.00
COWZ	Pacer US Cash Cows 100 ETF	$24,308,400.00

SPDW	SPDR Portfolio Developed World ex-US ETF	$23,954,300.00
USMV	iShares MSCI USA Min Vol Factor ETF	$23,793,700.00
JEPQ	JPMorgan NASDAQ Equity Premium Income ETF	$23,171,200.00
SHY	iShares 1-3 Year Treasury Bond ETF	$23,124,300.00
TQQQ	ProShares UltraPro QQQ	$22,866,400.00
MDY	SPDR S&P Midcap 400 ETF Trust	$22,802,700.00
JAAA	Janus Henderson AAA CLO ETF	$22,105,200.00

VGSH	Vanguard Short-Term Treasury ETF	$21,993,700.00
XLY	Consumer Discretionary Select Sector SPDR Fund	$21,906,400.00
XLC	Communication Services Select Sector SPDR Fund	$21,902,200.00
BIV	Vanguard Intermediate-Term Bond ETF	$21,898,900.00
IGSB	iShares 1-5 Year Investment Grade Corporate Bond ETF	$21,600,000.00
SMH	VanEck Semiconductor ETF	$21,112,900.00
EFV	iShares MSCI EAFE Value ETF	$20,943,700.00

VXF	Vanguard Extended Market ETF	$20,789,600.00
XLI	Industrial Select Sector SPDR Fund	$20,716,900.00
VGK	Vanguard FTSE Europe ETF	$20,585,200.00
SDY	SPDR S&P Dividend ETF	$20,358,000.00
IUSG	iShares Core S&P U.S. Growth ETF	$20,306,400.00
IUSV	iShares Core S&P U.S. Value ETF	$20,231,900.00
VMBS	Vanguard Mortgage-Backed Securities ETF	$20,010,500.00
DVY	iShares Select Dividend ETF	$19,811,700.00

| USHY | iShares Broad USD High Yield Corporate Bond ETF | $19,468,200.00 |

Top Brokerage Firms

BROKERAGE FIRM	ASSETS UNDER MANAGEMENT
Vanguard Group	$10.1 trillion
Charles Schwab	$10.1 trillion
UBS	$5.9 trillion
Fidelity Investments	$5.8 trillion
JPMorgan Chase & Co.	$4.05 trillion

Top Online Trading Brokerage Firms

Fidelity Investments

Charles Schwab

Ally Invest

E-trade

Firstrade

Interactive Brokers

Merrill Edge

Webull

Epilogue

One of the best ways to realize the purposeful apex of reading, *"Think Rich Act Rich Get Rich"* is for you to give your life to Christ Jesus. Repeat these simple words, and it will become a reality. Repeat the following: Lord Christ Jesus, as of this very moment, I accept you as Lord and Savior of my life. I now give my life to you so it can be fashioned for your purpose and glory. God, I believe everything I've said and confessed to you. I know now that I have received everlasting life based on the work that Christ has done and will continue to do in my life. Jesus, thank you for bringing me to this point where I surrender everything to you. It is in the Holy Spirit through Christ Jesus; I say Amen.

Humbly Yours in Christ

Book Dr. Jamie Pleasant for a
Speaking Engagement!

For speaking engagements, please contact Dr. Jamie T. Pleasant at admin@newzionchristianchurch.org or 678.845.7055

About the Author

Apostle Jamie T. Pleasant, Ph.D., a modern-day polymath, is the founder and Chief Executive Pastor of New Zion Christian Church in Suwanee, Georgia. Additionally, he is the former dean of graduate education and currently serves as a tenured Full Professor of Marketing at Clark Atlanta University's School of Business. Notably, he is the first faculty member in the university's history to be accepted into Mensa International, the world's largest and oldest high IQ society for individuals who have scored in the 98th percentile or above on an intelligence test.

Dr. Pleasant is the first African American to graduate from the Georgia Institute of Technology (Georgia Tech) with a Ph.D. in Business Management with a concentration in Marketing, earning that degree in August 1999. He is a 2016 recipient of the "Lifetime Achievement Award" from former President Barack Obama of the USA for volunteer and community service. He was awarded the "Game Changer" Educator Award by Reverend Jesse Jackson at the 2019 Rainbow PUSH International Convention. As a polyhistor, in addition to obtaining a doctorate degree in Business Management from the Georgia Institute of Technology, he holds a bachelor's degree in physics from Benedict College in Columbia, South Carolina, Marketing Studies from Clemson University and an M.B.A. in Marketing from the very prestigious, Clark Atlanta University.

Under his leadership, New Zion has grown from three members when it started in 1995 to well over 700 in weekly attendance, with a focus on economic and entrepreneurial development. God gave him the vision to establish a Biblically based economic development initiative for New Zion Christian Church. He remains at the pulse of the economic business sector in society.

As a result, Apostle Pleasant is in constant demand to train, speak and teach others at all levels in ministry and the private sector about business and economic development across the country. He has created numerous cutting edge and industry leading ministerial, business and economic development classes and programs, along with SAT & PSAT prep courses for children ages 9-19. He founded The Financial Literacy Academy for Youth (FLAFY), where youth between the ages of 13-19 attend 12-week intense classes on financial money management principles. At the end of those 12 weeks, they receive a "Personal Finance" certificate of achievement. In 2015, he established The Young Leadership and Success Academy that teaches young people between the ages of 10-21 how to invest, make presentations and start and operate businesses. Other ministries he has pioneered include The Wealth Builders Investment Club (WBIC), which educates and allows members to actively invest in the stock market, along with the much-celebrated Institute of Entrepreneurship (IOE), where participants earn a certificate in entrepreneurship after three months of comprehensive training in all aspects of starting and owning a successful competitive business. The main goal and purpose of IOE is that each year one of the trained businesses will be awarded up to $10,000 startup money to ensure financial success.

Apostle Pleasant has met with political officials such as former President Bill Clinton and Nelson Mandela. He has performed marriage ceremonies and counseled numerous celebrated personalities such as Usher Raymond, Terri Vaughn, and many others. Several gospel music artists have performed at the church, including Tiff Joy. Each year, Apostle Pleasant conducts chapel services for Clemson University's football team and is a spiritual and personal friend to its two-time national championship head coach, Dabo Swinney.

As a modern-day civil rights leader, he is a close aide to Reverend Jesse Jackson and serves on the Board of Directors of Rainbow PUSH Inc. (Atlanta) and Director of Business Education and Corporate Engagement. He serves on the Board of Fellowship of Christian Athletes (Atlanta Urban) and after the

Columbine High School shooting, he founded the National School Safety Advocacy Association. His latest foundations include the Young Entrepreneurship Program (YEP) and the African American Consumer Economic Rights (AACER).

He has authored numerous books that include: *Poems in the Verse of Life, Healing from the Loss of a Loved One, Trusting God In Troubling Times, Prayer Changes Things, Powerful Prayers That Open Heaven, Capturing and Keeping the Pastor's Heart, Unshakable Faith, Proverbs for Prosperity, How to release Your Blessings Through Service in Ministry, When Purpose is at Work, Today's Apostles (2024 ed.), Advertising Principles: How to Effectively Reach African Americans in the 21st Century, Discover a New You: A 21 Day Journey to Uncovering Your Uniqueness, Daily Quotes for Daily Blessings, The Making of a Man, I'm Just Sayin', From My Heart To Yours: Love Letters From A Loving Father, Today's Apostle: Servants of God Leading His People towards Unity, A 7 Day Prayer Plan for Prosperity, You Have*

What It Takes, A Marketing Model for Ethnic Consumer Behavior, An Overview of Strategic Healthcare Marketing and The Importance of Subcultural Marketing.

Apostle Pleasant is a lifetime member of Alpha Phi Alpha Fraternity Inc. He is the loving husband of the pulchritudinous Kimberly Pleasant and the proud father of three children: Christian, Zion and Nacara.

FINI